MANILA
THE CITY AT A GLANCE

The Gramercy Residences
This Gotham-esque winged and s[...]
by architects Roger Villarosa bec[...]
tallest residential building, at 25[...]
See p042

RCBC Plaza Yuchengco Tower
Designed by SOM, the shiny oval edifice is 46 storeys of blue glass, containing offices and an art museum. Behind, the fin of Kohn Pedersen Fox's GT Tower (Ayala Avenue) reaches 217m.
6813 Ayala Avenue

Club Intramuros Golf Course
One of the best situated urban courses in the world has 360-degree views of historic Manila.
See p094

National Museum
Both arms of this fine institution — the National Art Gallery and the Museum of the Filipino People — will stand you in good stead.
See p026

Waterfront Pavilion Hotel
The former Hilton, designed by Filipino Carlos Arguelles and opened in 1968, is part of an arresting modernist enclave on UN Avenue.
United Nations Avenue

Rizal Park
Soon after occupation, the US superimposed its homegrown urban framework on Manila. Centred on the ceremonial Rizal Park, it is characterised by wide avenues and imposing architecture that now houses state museums.

Mayfair Tower
Ermita and Malate are full of high-rise condos. This one spurns the usual des-res helicopter pad for a huge sky garden 132m above the bay.
526 United Nations Avenue

INTRODUCTION
THE CHANGING FACE OF THE URBAN SCENE

Asia's most underrated capital is often regarded as no more than a stopover en route to the Philippines' 7,107 islands. Yet, today, with foreign investment pouring in, a president tackling corruption and talented *balikbayans* returning home, it is cosmopolitan, dynamic and, yes, unpredictable, but a destination in its own right. On the street there is a palpable sense of excitement. The city is rising fast, in every sense, and many of the major architects are homegrown; from those dreaming up the shiny towers to the talent behind the restaurants, galleries and boutiques launching with aplomb – not to mention the furniture design, which has long been exemplary.

Sure, it's a confounding megalopolis and a headache to traverse. Not least because locals still don't recognise it as one entity (its 17 districts were unified in 1975) – confusingly referring to Intramuros as Manila, suburbs as 'villages' and boroughs as 'cities', even as new towns and super-malls proliferate. This guide, though, is all you need to negotiate the urban patchwork – apart from a helicopter. However much the city transforms, the heart remains its people, who are engaging, generous and truly hospitable. Natural disasters regularly beset the country yet Filipinos simply rebuild and bounce back. It's this spirit and resilience that make it unique, and Manila a success story in waiting. Let the unimaginative go to their desert paradise. They have no idea what they're missing. There is more adventure to be had in this vivid transcultural melange.

ESSENTIAL INFO
FACTS, FIGURES AND USEFUL ADDRESSES

TOURIST OFFICE
Room 106
Department of Tourism Building
TM Kalaw Street
T 525 2000
www.itsmorefuninthephilippines.com

TRANSPORT
Airport transfer to city centre
The official yellow airport taxis offer more reliable fares and drivers than other cabs, and are worth the often long wait. The journey to Makati costs PHP500
Car hire
Europcar Makati
T 752 7468
www.europcar.com
Rail transit system
www.trainguide.ph
Trains run from roughly 5am to 9.30pm
Taxi
www.grabtaxi.com
It's best to call for a cab or go to a rank

EMERGENCY SERVICES
Emergencies
T 117
24-hour pharmacy
Mercury Drug
32nd Street/4th Avenue, Fort
T 846 3417

EMBASSIES
British Embassy
120 Upper McKinley Road
T 858 2200
www.gov.uk/government/world/philippines
US Embassy
1201 Roxas Boulevard
T 301 2000
manila.usembassy.gov

POSTAL SERVICES
Post office
Magallanes Drive
T 525 7028
Shipping
UPS
411 Juan Luna Street
T 480 0048

BOOKS
Philippine Style: Design & Architecture
by Luca Tettoni and Elizabeth V Reyes
(Anvil Publishing)
Soledad's Sister by Jose Dalisay
(Anvil Publishing)

WEBSITES
Art
www.ncca.gov.ph
Culture
www.culturalcenter.gov.ph
Newspaper
www.philstar.com

EVENTS
Art Fair Philippines
www.artfairphilippines.com
Manila FAME
www.manilafame.com

COST OF LIVING
Taxi from Ninoy Aquino International Airport to Makati
PHP500
Cappuccino
PHP150
Packet of cigarettes
PHP75
Daily newspaper
PHP20
Bottle of champagne
PHP5,000

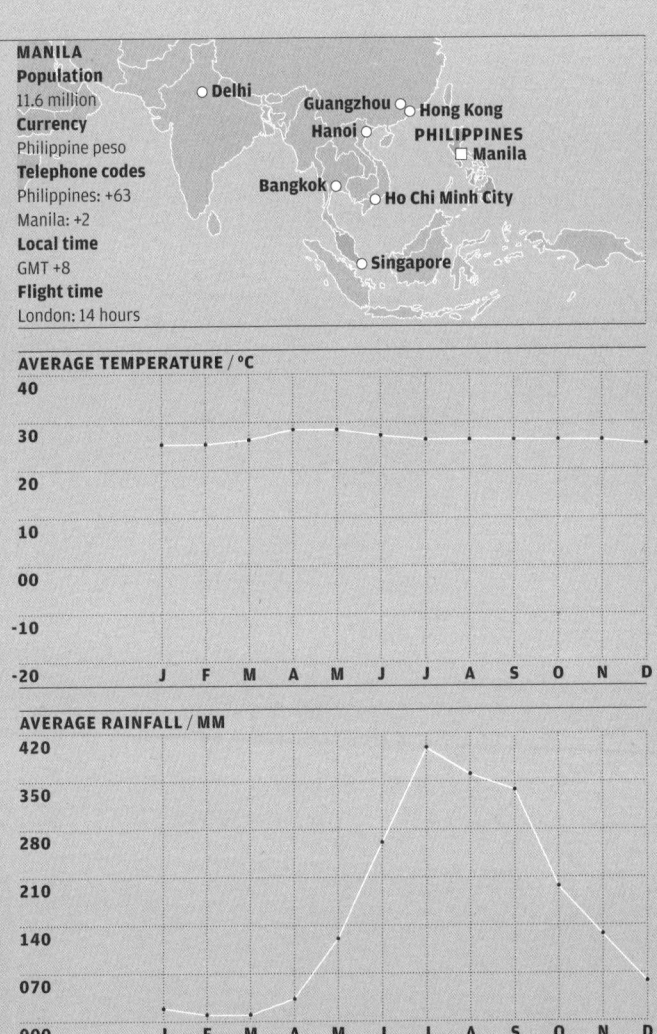

MANILA
Population
11.6 million
Currency
Philippine peso
Telephone codes
Philippines: +63
Manila: +2
Local time
GMT +8
Flight time
London: 14 hours

NEIGHBOURHOODS
THE AREAS YOU NEED TO KNOW AND WHY

To help you navigate the city, we've chosen the most interesting districts (see below and the map inside the back cover) and colour-coded our featured venues, according to their location; those venues that are outside these areas are not coloured.

MAKATI
Among the gleaming glass of the country's financial centre are quiet pockets like the laidback villages of Legazpi and Salcedo, and singular architecture such as Gabriel Formoso's Asian Institute of Management (123 Paseo de Roxas), dating to 1970, and the 1968 St Andrew the Apostle church (Nicanor Garcia Street) by Leandro Locsin.

QUEZON CITY
The purpose-built capital of the Philippines (from 1948 to 1976) contains government departments, monuments (see p011) and two universities. The students lend QC an unpretentious feel, encapsulated at unique venues like restaurant Van Gogh is Bipolar (154 Maginhawa, T 922 824 3051).

BINONDO/QUIAPO
Over the bridge from Intramuros, Binondo is the world's oldest Chinatown, settled from 1594. Escolta Street (see p076) was lined with art deco boutiques in the 1930s, but lost its lustre long ago. Head to Quiapo for Malacañang Palace (see p024) and the Basilica of San Sebastian (see p064).

PASAY/MALL OF ASIA
To give an idea of the scale of the city's retail landscape, the Mall of Asia was the 11th-largest shopping centre in the world in 2014, but only third-largest in Manila. Pasay is more cultured, exemplified by Locsin's CCP (see p012), and the Sofitel (see p020), popular for sunset cocktails.

FORT
Towers are topping out fast in Manila's newest district, also known as Bonifacio Global City. Two of the most hyped are IM Pei's Essensa East Forbes (21st Drive) and Arquitectonica's Pacific Plaza Towers (4th Avenue), home to Imelda and seemingly crowned by UFOs. Office blocks house chic restaurants such as Vask (see p052).

INTRAMUROS/RIZAL PARK
Manila was founded here in 1571, and the walled city of Intramuros is a tourist draw despite the baroque San Agustin Church (General Luna Street, T 527 4060) being the only building of note to survive WWII. Locals refer to Rizal Park as Luneta and come for family picnics and first dates.

ORTIGAS
This has been a vital business district since the 1970s; brave the traffic to admire the corporate temples of San Miguel (see p070) and Meralco (see p074). Shop for upscale and international brands at The Podium (12 ADB Avenue) and Shangri-La Plaza (EDSA/Shaw Boulevard, T 370 2500).

ERMITA/MALATE
The heart of the party scene in the 1970s, Malate has maintained a bohemian vibe, experienced at venues like The Bar @ 1951 (1951 M Adriatico Street) and the North Syquia apartments (see p085). Ermita's highlight is the collection of midcentury offices along UN Avenue (see p069).

LANDMARKS
THE SHAPE OF THE CITY SKYLINE

A conurbation of 17 sub-cities, Manila is often unfathomable. It was razed in WWII but has grown exponentially since. The port at the mouth of the Pasig, the Spanish core and the US influence centred on Rizal Park have long been left behind. Indeed, Manila seems to have simply abandoned its past and its heritage, and run amok.

A purpose-built capital was established postwar in Quezon City, full of monuments (see p011) and state buildings, but what most stands out today is the overblown gothic revival Iglesia ni Cristo (Commonwealth Avenue), a temple complex on a hill, that's almost the size of the Vatican, demonstrating the importance of religion in the Philippines. From here, you can see that navigation is easy enough on a macro scale thanks to isolated clusters of skyscrapers on the flat landscape that mark a series of satellite towns – but once you're actually there, the high-rises can be disorienting.

Ortigas is signposted by the Meralco Building (see p074) and condos like the 55-storey BSA Twin Towers (Julia Vargas Avenue), garishly lit at night. In Makati and Fort, super-towers (see p014) dwarf the rest of Manila. Due to commutes that take in back alleys and nondescript highways, combined with a city in flux, it's easy to get lost. Locals use small-scale reference points. When stuck in traffic, look out the window at the billboard, tell them the celebrity and the product, and they'll know exactly how late you'll be.
For full addresses, see Resources.

Manila Post Office

Commanding the Pasig since 1926, the MPO was created in perfect neoclassical symmetry by Ralph Doane, Tomás Mapúa and Juan Marcos Arellano. Destroyed in WWII, it was rebuilt in 1946 to the initial design. The location was chosen because the river was once a busy artery, weaving 25km from the port to Laguna de Bay, until siltation, pollution and the humble water lily intervened, although a ferry service was relaunched in 2014 in a bid to ease road congestion. The building still serves its original function, a cartoon-like statue of a postman waving a letter at the rear, but the government is considering proposals by Singapore's Fullerton group to convert it into a hotel. Next door is the Bauhaus-style National Press Club by Angel Nakpil, completed in 1955.
Magallanes Drive

Quezon Memorial Circle

This site, in the centre of a 25-hectare park, from which roads fan out in all directions, was earmarked for the National Capitol before the war, but plans were changed to create a mausoleum for president Manuel L Quezon, who died in 1944. Federico S Ilustre won the commission in 1951 but work was held up by inept management and the cost of importing marble, and it was only finished 27 years on. Three 66m pylons symbolising the nation's geography are topped by angels sculpted by Francesco Monti; bas-reliefs at the base were added in the 1980s. Inside, a museum displays presidential memorabilia. Near the park, check out the modernist Quezon City Hall (Elliptical Road) and, around East Avenue, the powerful Philippine Heart Center and International Style SSS Building.
Elliptical Road

Cultural Center of the Philippines

The 1969 CCP is the pièce de résistance in a brutalist cultural ensemble by Leandro Locsin on 77 hectares of reclaimed land. Inspired by indigenous houses on stilts, a massive cantilevered slab faced in marble appears to float on its concave concrete columns. Ramps sweep around a fountain and sculpture garden to the theatres and galleries. Elsewhere in the complex, the Folk Arts Theater was built in 77 days for the 1974 Miss Universe pageant (when a typhoon hit, coconuts were nailed back on to trees), and the Manila Film Center was rushed through for a 1982 festival, many workers dying when a roof collapsed. The monumental buildings were criticised as propaganda to distract from corruption allegations against the Marcoses but their architectural beauty is unquestionable.
Roxas Boulevard, www.culturalcenter.gov.ph

013

LANDMARKS

Discovery Primea

The late Japanese architect Kenzo Tange's final project and his first in the Philippines, a partnership with Jorge Ramos, opened in 2014. As part of a new crop of residential towers, it's a powerful symbol of where the city is heading. Not only up physically, but metaphorically too – premium real estate and plenty of superlatives to attract the big spenders – especially considering that as recently as the 1960s, this was all farmland. Primea stands out not just for its height but the yellow granite facade and unconventional steps and terraces. A 15-floor base houses 141 upscale serviced 'hotel' suites (T 955 8888) with kitchens, and the slender tower has 90 apartments, two per storey. There are pools, a spa, bars and restaurants, all topped by a helipad.
6749 Ayala Avenue,
www.discoveryprimea.com

Manila Hotel

The US sought to impose itself on Manila through urban planning to a blueprint by Daniel Burnham (responsible for Chicago and San Francisco). Man on the ground William Parsons melded Spanish colonial designs (adapted to the tropical climate) with neoclassicism. This is exemplified in the 1912 Manila Hotel, its marble lobby featuring Doric columns, a narra-wood ceiling, mahogany furniture and capiz-shell chandeliers. The H-shaped plan was redeveloped in 1976 and a tower added. There are now 550 rooms with some fine views, although those of the container port may not be among them. The Champagne Room is no longer a high-society haunt but the foyer is still a hubbub of excitement for tour groups and congress delegates.
One Rizal Park, T 527 0011, www.manila-hotel.com.ph

HOTELS

WHERE TO STAY AND WHICH ROOMS TO BOOK

The Philippines has long been a tourist draw, but certainly not with Manila as its star. And due to a paradise-seeking clientele who treat the capital as a necessary evil, an influx of foreign executives, and an affluent local market that loves a staycation, accommodation here is safe and reliable – big brands, big properties. The boutique concept barely registers at all, although the odd block of serviced apartments (see p018) provides a more tailored experience.

In the mid-1970s, the Marcoses funded showcase hotels, and thanks to a succession of renovations, The Pen (see p023) and the Sofitel (see p020) are still as relevant today. Along with the ever-reliable Makati Shangri-La (Ayala Avenue/Makati Avenue, T 813 8888), which arrived in 1993, there was little choice beyond these behemoths. However, a renaissance is underway as Makati shoots skywards – Raffles and Fairmont (see p022) share a glass box, and ostentatious suites can now be reserved in Discovery Primea (see p014). In Fort, a Shangri-La and a Grand Hyatt will be unveiled in 2015, both in soaring 250m towers, while the Marco Polo (Meralco Avenue/Sapphire Street, T 720 7777) opened in Ortigas. Continuing the build-it-and-they-will-come mentality is the mammoth Vegas-style development on the bay. Solaire (opposite) was joined by the first Nobu (City of Dreams, T 866 9888) in Asia in 2014, with more resorts and casinos planned, including a Conrad in the Mall of Asia. *For full addresses and room rates, see Resources.*

Solaire Resort & Casino

When it debuted in 2013, in the greenfield government-sponsored Entertainment City, many agreed with Solaire's tagline that 'the game has changed'. The Paul Steelman-designed resort certainly looks the US$1bn it cost to build, from the 500 luxe rooms to 18,500 sq m of gaming space. The two-bedroom bayside villas, including the Chairman's Villa (Master Bedroom, above), each have a pool, jacuzzi and terrace, set in prime position for majestic views of the sunset. There's also a fine selection of restaurants (see p050) and impressive Filipino and international art, most of it museum quality, such as the abstract resin paintings by Matthew James, a BenCab brass sculpture at the VIP entrance and 3D installations by Antonio Arcellana.
1 Asean Avenue, Entertainment City, T 888 8888, www.solaireresort.com

Picasso Boutique Serviced Apartments

Architect Dominic Galicia and interior designer Tina Periquet have taken cubism to heart in their 2009 conversion of this residential block, most ingeniously in the facade. From a side view, the painted walls of the square recessed balconies coalesce to reveal a composite image of a woman. Inside, there are 136 spacious apartments, equipped with kitchenettes; the two 93 sq m lofts (Picasso, above) have mezzanines and floating staircases, and are great for entertaining. Interiors are characterised by art deco-style furniture, bold colour blocks and framing devices. Most of the art, which is by local talent throughout (and can also be seen in the bijou gallery), is for sale. The company also runs Joya Lofts (T 798 0497) in the Rockwell Center.
119 LP Leviste Street, T 828 4774, www.picassomakati.com

Sofitel Philippine Plaza
Part of Locsin's CCP ensemble (see p012), the Philippine Plaza has stood on the bay since 1976. Two stepped concrete blocks are distinguished by recessed balconies that allow alfresco views from each of the 609 rooms. A low-slung flat-canopied entrance leads down a sweeping staircase to the lauded Spiral restaurant (pictured), which serves a formidable smorgasbord of global cuisine, and a huge organic pool and gardens landscaped by Ildefonso P Santos. Rooms, renovated by HOK, are detailed with coconut inlays, capiz shell lamps, mother-of-pearl and wicker – the Corner Suites have dual-aspect terraces. The resort also has a multilevel spa (T 551 1587), tennis courts and jogging paths; and despite its size, service is faultless. *CCP Complex, Roxas Boulevard, T 551 5555, www.sofitelmanila.com*

Raffles

The all-suite Raffles is ensconced on the ninth and tenth floors of a 30-storey glass tower, designed by Arquitectonica, that opened in 2012 and also houses the bigger, business-oriented Fairmont Hotel. The two share restaurants and facilities, and are distinguished by the colour of the marble flooring, although Raffles has its own roof garden and infinity pool (above) and is a treasure trove of Philippine art, which was commissioned for the hotel. Its 32 large suites have wood floors, tactile materials such as satin, silk and damask, and great views – the best are of the Greenbelt mall. Naturally, the Long Bar, which is furnished with a mural of boxer Manny Pacquiao, has its own version of the Singapore Sling, the Makati Sling, topped with gold flakes.
1 Raffles Drive, Makati Avenue, T 555 9777, www.raffles.com/makati

The Peninsula

The Marcoses bankrolled The Peninsula to impress delegates attending the 1976 IMF conference, and Gabriel Formoso's soaring lobby still does a fine job, although its neoclassical pomp is out of kilter with the semi-brutalist concrete wings. Napoleón Abueva's 12m *Sunburst* sculpture on the ceiling was installed in 1994, and the army ram-raided the front doors with a tank to quash a coup in 2007; this history ensures its popularity for *merienda*. On weekends, especially Fridays, locals 'free flow' in the bar on the all-you-can-drink deals, and, next-door, Salon de Ning club is modelled on a 1930s Shanghai opium den. The Pen's 493 stylishly updated rooms and suites (Deluxe, above) are dressed with Filipino weavings and seashell lampshades.
Ayala Avenue/Makati Avenue, T 887 2888, www.peninsula.com/manila

24 HOURS
SEE THE BEST OF THE CITY IN JUST ONE DAY

The biggest challenge in Manila is beating the hellish traffic. The city might have super-highways but they're invariably gridlocked until 9pm, made worse by plagues of motorbikes. Public transport is lamentable, and although taxis are cheap and plentiful, they are almost always busy. At least smartphone apps like GrabTaxi and Uber have made getting around more convenient, reliable and safe.

You could easily fill 24 hours with a different itinerary to the one here (except on Monday when places close). The Metropolitan Museum (Roxas Boulevard, T 708 7828) combines ancient gold and modern art. Get a historical outline at the 1750 Malacañang Palace (1000 JP Laurel Street, T 784 4286), and a glimpse of the Marcoses' bizarre life at Marikina Shoe Museum (JP Rizal Street, T 646 2368), which has 800 pairs of Imelda's shoes. Then head to the tropical modernist University of the Philippines (Diliman), laid out by Juan Nakpil in 1948. The highlight is Locsin's 1955 Church of the Holy Sacrifice – a concrete dome on pillars with a B-movie vibe – and work by Napoleón Abueva, Vicente Manansala and Ang Kiukok.

Find a vantage point to watch the sunset before dining Filipino-style on the 12-course degustation menu at Pepita's Kitchen (1050 Magallanes Avenue, T 425 4605) in owner Dedet de la Fuente's front room. Or book the 'secret' table suspended on a mezzanine in Black Sheep (see p039) for a superlative taste of contemporary Manila. *For full addresses, see Resources.*

08.30 Hatch 22

French-Filipino siblings Erwan and Solenn Heussaff's all-day dining concept opens for breakfast at 7am and ends with cocktails, until 1am at weekends. The space reflects this transition, starting with the aroma of the bakery as you enter, and following the long wooden slats of the undulating ceiling that segue from an open, vertical position to closed and horizontal towards the back. Interiors display graphic mosaic tiles, and art by Solenn. As the sun streams through the windows, start the day with the three reimagined Filipino staples (*tocino*, *tapa* and corned beef), or the Not Your Ordinary Benedicts (NYOB) with sous-vide eggs, and a single-origin coffee. A good alternative for breakfast if you're in Fort is Wildflour Cafe + Bakery (see p051).
Power Plant Mall, Rockwell Drive/ Estrella Street, T 915 109 7711

10.00 National Museum

Rizal Park is surrounded by pastel-hued neoclassical giants. Antonio Toledo and US architect Ralph Harrington Doane's 1926 library was reconfigured to house the senate, but was mostly destroyed in WWII. It was reconstructed postwar and, in 1996, converted into the National Art Gallery, which covers pieces from the 18th century onwards by the likes of Carlos Francisco, José Rizal and Gene Cabrera. The Old Senate Session Hall was restored in 2012, and soars three storeys with Corinthian columns and murals by Juan Marcos Arellano. Below, in the Hall of Masters, is the country's most famous painting, Juan Luna's *Spoliarium* (1884). The Museum of the Filipino People is in the old Department of Finance next door.
*Padre Burgos Drive, T 527 0278,
www.nationalmuseum.gov.ph*

11.30 Artelano 11
Behind a red gate on an acacia-lined street near Pasay, this compound of 1950s white wooden houses set in sculpture-strewn landscaped gardens has beautiful period details, not least the rich *machuca* tiles. Artelano 11 comprises four connected properties, the foil for Eric Paras' eclectic collection of art deco- and midcentury-inspired pieces, some of which he designs himself, as well as reimagined Filipino craft and home accessories sourced from across Asia. It's a melting pot of ideas, from French crockery to porcelain jars, cheeseboards made out of flattened wine bottles and handcarved headboards. Also in the creative enclave is Avellana Art Gallery (T 833 8357), which specialises in abstract and folk art, and fashion designer Jojie Lloren's atelier (T 556 4725).
2680 FB Harrison Street, T 832 9972

12.30 M Café

Museum Café, affectionately known as M, draws the creative set on Thursday, Friday and Saturday nights when DJs spin and the party spills on to the plaza. But it's a fine spot at any time for modern Asian cuisine, such as smoked milkfish salad and Szechuan-style crab. Cocktails highlight local ingredients like *lambanog* (coconut wine), pomelo, honey and pandan-infused rum. Budji Layug + Royal Pineda's design incorporates custom furniture, Bertjan Pot's 'Random Light' pendants and paper installations by Tes Pasola. Sharing the premises is Filipino restaurant Kabila, where dishes like seafood guava *sinigang* are served creatively. Afterwards, check out Greenbelt Mall's delightful open-air Santo Niño de Paz Chapel (T 729 8173). *Ground floor, Greenbelt 4, Makati Avenue, T 757 6000, www.raintreerestaurants.com*

13.15 Ayala Museum

Envisioned in the 1950s by abstract painter Fernando Zóbel, the museum came to life thanks to the financial muscle of the Ayala Group, which owns huge swathes of Makati. In 2004, it moved to this angular building of green glass, steel and stone by Leandro Locsin Junior. Its striking lobby of Angola black and travertine marble and a four-storey floating staircase is used for events. Permanent exhibits focus on ethnography, archaeology and iconography, and art by the Filipino masters Juan Luna, Fernando Amorsolo and, of course, Zóbel. Temporary shows, such as Elmer Borlongan's 'In City and Country' (above), are often of more interest, ranging from retrospectives to contemporary visual artists and touring international stars like Ai Weiwei.
Greenbelt 4, Makati Avenue, T 759 8288, www.ayalamuseum.org

15.00 Kenneth Cobonpue

Eschewing the Filipino trait of *boiloloy* (over-design) — exhibit A, the psychedelic jeepney — Cebu-based Kenneth Cobonpue's graceful creations are inspired by nature and crafted from indigenous materials like rattan, abaca and bamboo. His 4,000 sq m showroom opened in 2013, the coldness of the poured concrete floors and unfinished walls highlighting the warm textures of his organic, witty designs. The 'Chiquita' stool is a bunch of poles that acts as a cushion; the 'Parchment' table's warped layers of wood evoke an ancient book; the sculptural 'Bloom' chair unfurls to resemble an arum lily; and the 'Tilt' chair (above) does just that. There is even talk of a bamboo car. It is a wonderfully inspiring space.
The Residences at Greenbelt, San Lorenzo Tower, Arnaiz Avenue, T 576 1639, www.kennethcobonpue.com

16.15 US Military Cemetery

A rolling 62-hectare plateau in Fort is the resting place of more than 17,000 soldiers who died in the Philippines and New Guinea during WWII. The largest overseas US military cemetery, it was inaugurated in 1960, and rows and rows of white marble crosses stretch across a huge lawn. In the centre is a chapel with a bas-relief of St George, and a wide circular limestone colonnade into which are etched the names of at least 36,000 missing in action, while sizeable mosaic maps detail key US battles in the Pacific, China, India and Burma. The serenity of the site is in stark contrast to the city's chaos – towers such as SM Aura Premier (far right; see p072) can be seen outside the gates – but there are also views out to Laguna de Bay and the mountains.
McKinley Road, T 844 0212

17.00 Art Informal
This converted 1960s residence is run by Tina Fernandez and Salvador Joel Alonday. It champions contemporary sculpture, painting and ceramics, plus installations, multimedia events and performances in three high-ceilinged spaces. The main room might feature emerging artists like Lui Medina ('Metamorphic Histories', left), while the Inner Room is an intimate setting for solo shows. Manila has a plethora of excellent private galleries, which all sell affordable art. Artist-run MO_Space (T 856 2748), in the MOs Design Building in Fort, is worth checking out for experimental works. Over in Ermita, 1335MABINI (T 254 8498) is a multidisciplinary venture in Casa Tesoro, a 1902 mansion displaying sculptures, textiles and Cordillera crafts; under its umbrella are the innovative art projects BAR and Zn Gallery.
227 Connecticut Street, Greenhills East, T 725 8518, www.artinformal.com

18.00 Artlab Atelier Syjuco
Cesare and Jean Marie Syjuco made their name as proponents of postmodernism in the 1980s, and their four-storey house is a repository of their work. It's 45 minutes out of town and visits must be arranged in advance, but it's a fascinating way to spend the afternoon. The couple are provocateurs who excel in installation, literary hybrids and performance art, and have a healthy appetite for the surreal. In their glass-fronted home, painted white and divided into mezzanines, artworks often become everyday objects, such as the *Forty Winks* bed. Paintings by Cesare include *Please Notice the Air* (above, top) and *Tipping in America* (a tank, firing, inscribed with 'Have a swell day'). Perched on high is his bust of a rotting Marilyn Monroe.
327 Country Club Drive, Ayala Alabang, T 917 534 0779

21.30 Black Sheep

In the penthouse of the colourfully tiled W Fifth Avenue, half of Black Sheep has superlative views of Fort. The rest of the space is expressly focused on eating and drinking. From a massive open kitchen, progressive Filipino chef Jordy Navarra orchestrates four-course set menus that include dishes such as Kitayama tenderloin (Wagyu from Bukidnon) cooked sous vide, blow-torched and paired with squid-ink mash. 'The philosophy is to capture the flavour spectrum of our people in one meal,' says Navarra. The whisky/cocktail bar serves the country's largest selection of single malts (suggested as pairings for dinner) and small plates like Mock Nuggets (black truffle, cauliflower and corn). On Fridays, DJs play deep house until 3am.
W Fifth Avenue, 32nd Avenue/5th Avenue, T 478 4498, www.blacksheepbgc.com

URBAN LIFE
CAFÉS, RESTAURANTS, BARS AND NIGHTCLUBS

As sophisticated Filipinos return from overseas in droves, lured by Manila's current dynamism, they all comment on how much has changed. A resurgence in Pinoy pride has fostered an appreciation of homegrown cuisine, which fuses Spanish, Malay, Chinese and US influences: restaurants like Mesa (see p053); Sarsa (Unit 1-7, Forum South Global, 7th Avenue, T 927 706 0773), overseen by *MasterChef* judge JP Anglo; and La Cocina de Tita Moning (315 San Rafael Street, T 734 2141), in a museum-like art deco home in the grounds of the presidential palace (see p024), are often full. Innovative chefs such as Jordy Navarra (see p039) are reviving an enthusiasm for local ingredients and developing culinary fusions.

There is also a flourishing third-wave coffee movement led by brewers like The Curator (opposite) and Craft Coffee Revolution (66 Broadway Avenue, T 570 3464). Bucketloads of San Miguel still fuel post-work drinking sessions but more Filipinos are cultivating a taste for the grape, at wine bars like CAV (see p059) and Ninyo Lounge (66 Esteban Abada Street, T 426 0301). The biggest craze, though, is for the speakeasy. Blind Pig (227 Salcedo Street, T 917 549 2264) germinated a cocktail culture by consulting a New York mixologist, and was followed by sister venture Exit (Corinthian Plaza, 121 Paseo de Roxas, T 551 1283) – accessed through the back of Plaza Cafe – and a host of other 'secret' hideaways.
For full addresses, see Resources.

The Curator
The expert team at The Curator show a reverence for both coffee and cocktails, manifested in a respect for the origins of every single ingredient, from beans to homemade bitters and small-batch spirits, including local liquors such as Don Papa rum. Their carefully concocted beverages fuel conversation at this difficult-to-find speakeasy-style back room tucked inside Cyrano Wine Bar. It might be a windowless concrete box, but it exudes intimacy and a sense of having stumbled upon a secret sect. A framed bar area, fashioned from salvaged wood, forms the 'stage' for the engaging mixologists to practise their art/science. The tight-knit group has since opened EDSA Beverage Design Group (T 917 859 005), a larger space that sells equipment and offers barista training.
134 Legaspi Street, T 917 893 7115

71 Gramercy

Perched 250m up in the air, this is quite literally a place to see – and be seen. Manila's in-crowd cram the lifts up to this destination restaurant, lounge and club that's decorated with leather walls, chesterfields, dozens of orb lights and a mirror-clad DJ booth. The outdoor deck and bar has a 360-degree panorama.
Gramercy Residences, Kalayaan Avenue/ Salamanca Street, T 917 847 7535

The Black Pig

Despite its low-key location in a mall in Alabang, 45 minutes from the centre, The Black Pig has been a huge success since opening in 2013, in large part due to chef Carlos Garcia, who perfected his craft at Gauthier Soho in London. As you'd expect, there's a devotion to pork here, especially Spanish Iberico and Philippine *lechón* (the national dish), although the menu also encompasses the likes of steamed black cod and black-ink risotto. Drink a Holgate craft beer on tap at the bar (above). Design HQ's Chako Hirayama and Jobele Tee used exposed brick, iron beams, mango-wood tables, leather upholstery, reproduction Edison light bulbs and geometric patterns to emulate the ambience of an urban loft. *Second floor, Commercenter Alabang, Commerce Avenue, Filinvest, Corporate City, T 808 1406, www.theblackpigbar.com*

Grace Park

Chef Margarita Forés named Grace Park after her ancestral home, and designed it with her architect cousin Jorge Yulo, using found or vintage objects. There's a wall of recycled brick; old Pizza Hut seats were refurbished with gold leaf; the gloriously mismatched glasses came from Kamuning market; and corrugated cardboard boxes turned into menus. This is a restaurant with a conscience, and a farm-to-table, seed-to-plate concept, promoting healthy, seasonal ingredients in dishes like organic Scotch eggs, vegetable tempura, pasta with squash, pistachio and goats' cheese, and muscovado beef belly. The best tables are at the front near the open kitchen or on the mezzanine, which has a lovely wrought-iron balcony. Forés also runs Lusso (T 756 5893) in Greenbelt 5.
One Rockwell Drive, T 843 7275

Prime 101
Up a spiral staircase on the second floor of a nondescript office building, Prime 101 (the '101' logo a fork, plate and knife) is a revelation. Wood-panelled doors open up to a furniture showroom/restaurant. This intimate living room has dark polished floors, plumped-up sofas, contemporary art and photography, and just seven tables surrounded by a collection of prototype chairs, many designed by partner Jennifer de Dios; all of the pieces are for sale. A chalkboard lists raw ingredients – cuts of steak, lamb or pork, and catches of the day – and you dictate the style of cuisine, be it Filipino, Korean or French, before freestyling chef Marco Legasto creates your own customised meal. For a starter, the foie gras dumplings stand out, and there's an excellent wine selection too.
2226 Chino Roces Street, T 720 8674

Wafu
Designed by Don Yeung, Anica De Guzman and Isabel Maniti, this sprawling Japanese spot is a melange of textures, from marble to rough-cut boulders and polished timber. Eyes are drawn, however, to the wire-mesh 'lotus pods' by Ann Pamintuan that offer some privacy within the bustle. Indulge in dishes such as wasabi tempura short ribs.
Greenhills Shopping Center, Ortigas Avenue, T 570 3242

Strip

Every restaurant interior within casino resort Solaire (see p017) hits the jackpot. Cantonese venue Red Lantern flaunts large-scale chinoiserie portraits by Bojo and Carmel Lim-Torres; Finestra (Italian) has cascading crystals and colour-blocked Louis XVI-inspired chairs; and the Dragon Bar centres on a sculpture made with more than 1,500 crystals. The steakhouse, Strip, has a masculine vibe due to its black granite floors and pillars, zebrano-wood panelling, a surreal carpet and a huge wine cellar. You get to choose a Laguiole knife to go with your 350g American prime rib-eye as well. There's a lot to be said for dining late in the afternoon as there's an outstanding view of Manila Bay, so you can watch the sunset, cognac in hand.
Solaire, 1 Asean Avenue, Entertainment City, T 888 8888, www.solaireresort.com

Wildflour Cafe + Bakery

When the cronut craze took off in the US, Wildflour created its own version almost immediately, and its ever-evolving pastry cabinet is testament to the bakery's desire to innovate. Previously, it was unheard of for Filipinos to wait for tables but only a few can be reserved here, so the lines are often long, although turnover is high. Wildflour champions a formula of comfort food, such as its dish Luke's Favorite (a slab of maple-glazed pork belly bacon with roast pear); cocktails like Bloody Mary Balsamico and Passionfruit Mimosa; and pimped-up teas including pistache au lait and honey soy latte. It's a casual, bustling space with thickset communal tables, a cherry-red banquette, chalkboard menus, high wooden ceilings and whitewashed brick: all the aesthetics of an LA bistro.
4th Avenue/26th Street, T 856 7600

Vask

Carlo Calma's playful CLIPP Center opened in 2013, its 12 storeys of glass covered in a mess of metal diagonal struts. On the fifth floor is Spanish restaurant and tapas bar, Vask, helmed by chef Jose Luis Gonzalez, who trained under Ferran Adrià, and the counter is laden with *pintxos* at cocktail hour. Interiors, also designed by Calma, are equally fun. The perforated ceiling of the dining room calls to mind emmental cheese, and the deck (above) has a cutlery theme – spoons as love seats and forks as lighting armatures. The art-laden Gallery Vask seats 20 for its multi-course tasting menus, and the whimsical Curve, a seafood lounge, has upside-down umbrella lights reflected in mirrored tables. There's even a map of Fort etched into wood in the lift.
Fifth floor, CLIPP Center, 11th Avenue/39th Street, T 217 6563, www.galleryvask.com

Mesa Filipino Moderne

The trademark at Mesa, a contemporary take on Filipino food in SM Aura Premier (see p072), is *crispchon* – pig skin wrapped in pandan crêpes with cucumber, spring onion, coriander and liver or hoisin sauce, and eaten Peking duck-style. Also wildly popular are the *laing* (taro leaves cooked in coconut milk and shrimp paste) and *hito* (catfish) with mango salad. The drink *halo-halo* (literally, 'hotchpotch') is truly a dessert in a glass. Carlo Calma's interior features sculptural dividers created using *sawali* weaving methods, lights modelled on farmers' hats and a sink inspired by the Banaue Rice Terraces. Other good spots in which to try local dishes are Abe Serendra (T 856 0526) and Aracama Filipino Cuisine (T 917 861 2702), both in Fort.
SM Aura Premier, C5 Road/26th Street, T 815 2872, www.mesa.ph

054

Las Flores

Spanish gastro-bar Las Flores specialises in modern tapas such as scallop ceviche, and unique cocktails like the Calamansi (lime spirit) and Cherry Blossom Mule. These are all delivered with superlative service inside an industrial/rustic design featuring floral clay tiles. There's a sister venue, Rambla (T 823 6468), at Rockwell. *One McKinley Place, 25th Street/ 4th Avenue, T 552 2815*

Privé Luxury Club
Manila's many nightspots attract a mainly young, college crowd. Legendary superclub Republiq (T 917 550 8888), by the airport, flies in DJs like Avicii, and Hyve (T 917 633 5882) is well located on the top of the W Global Center, but the stylish set head to 71 Gramercy (see p042) or the 'boutique' Privé. It's as plush as you'd expect, with velvet, gold and mirrored walls, tufted couches, flock wallpaper and chandeliers; bottle service is popular. To a soundtrack of house and pop, the party starts after midnight when Manileños earn their *loco* reputation – and as the selfie capital of the world, it will all be documented on Instagram. Filipinos also love to sing, and a night out often means wielding a mic at karaoke palaces like Red Box (T 757 6188). *Unit C, The Fort Strip, T 917 898 8181, www.priveluxuryclub.com*

Recess by Chef Chris
Taking the school break-time as a theme, interior designer Noel Bernardo did his homework, dreaming up a periodic table for a ceiling, steel-and-wood fixtures that give Recess a classroom feel, accents of bright colours, lockers against one wall and a clock that is permanently stopped at 10.30am. Swiss chef Chris Locher is renowned for 'inventing' *panizzas* – thin-slice pizza in flavour combinations such as beef, bacon, pineapple and mushrooms, cut into strips and topped with rocket and alfalfa sprouts that are rolled into a cylinder before eating. They are the main attraction here, although there are also canteen-style dishes such as pastas and burgers. Polaroids of customers fill up one wall. It's very (old) school and a generous helping of Filipino fun.
50 Jupiter Street, Bel-Air, T 899 1818

Sala

A survivor of the 1990s Remedios dining scene, Sala was an oasis of sophistication in a sea of boisterous bars. Scottish chef Colin Mackay relocated his fine-dining European restaurant to Makati in 2007, as the city's centre of gravity shifted, and it has gone from strength to strength, thanks to dishes such as twice-baked soufflé with prawns, feta and dill. In a dramatic space softened by ebony veneer and smoked mirrors, it fronts a terrace in the 1987 LV Locsin Building, designed by the architect himself, a 19-floor brutalist tower defined by its parallel concrete balconies and lack of corner columns – a feature flaunted in the staircases when lit up at night. Mackay also runs Sala Bistro (T 729 4888) and Thai restaurant People's Palace (T 729 2888).
Podium level, 6752 Ayala Avenue, T 750 5159, www.salarestaurant.com

CAV

When it opened in 2007, CAV was the first place in Manila to offer the Enomatic wine dispensing system, with 24 bottles. Today, the retail store/café/fine-dining concept, designed by Noel Bernardo, carries more than 450 labels, including the coveted 1997 Screaming Eagle from Napa Valley. The setting is all industrial chic, via a chunky timber-beamed ceiling, concrete floors, blackboard menus and barrels for tables in the casual area. The colour palette becomes more muted in the restaurant, which has whitewashed brick walls and mosaic tile features, and chef Markus Gfeller's menu turns fancier in dishes like seared foie gras on celeriac panna cotta, and black cod topped with slow-cooked octopus and salmon roe garnish.
Lot 5, Quadrant 8, Bonifacio High Street, T 856 1798, www.cavwine.com

Black Market

In a part of Makati populated by galleries and ad agencies, and at the vanguard of a new wave of underground venues, Black Market is an industrial-style indie club run by the folks behind party and gig venue B-Side (see p081) at The Collective. It is a raw, dark warehouse space in which diagonal wood slats create odd angles and form a mezzanine and sky bridge leading to a wall of street art. Behind a black door near the entrance is the speakeasy Finders Keepers (T 555 5555), illuminated only by its red neon sign and candles. In a living-room atmosphere, bartenders in bow ties and braces mix craft cocktails. The Spice of Life (tequila, vodka and Cointreau) has quite a kick – best not to balance on the built-in swing while drinking it. Alleviate the munchies at Joe's Meat Shack in a repurposed shipping container outside.
Warehouse 5, La Fuerza/Compound 2, Sabio Street, T 908 813 5622

URBAN LIFE

INSIDER'S GUIDE
JESSICA KIENLE, FURNITURE DESIGNER

Swiss-Filipina Jessica Kienle returned to the Philippines from the US in 2012. 'It's an exciting time to be here,' says the head designer of family furniture firm Philux. 'There's a different energy. Manila is changing into a global city as cultures merge.' This is apparent in the restaurants she frequents, from Filipino cuisine at Romulo Café (148 Jupiter Street, Bel-Air, T 478 6406) to Thai at People's Palace (see p058), neo-Japanese at Kai (Greenbelt 5, T 757 5209), Chinese at Red Lantern (see p050), where Kienle loves the dim sum brunch, and Italian at Caruso (21 Nicanor Garcia Street, T 895 2451): 'You'd think you were in Rome.' On a night out, she's a fan of cocktails at Niner Ichi Nana (The Globe Tower, 32nd Street, T 917 876 9999), the ornate Salon de Ning (see p023) and the cosy Blind Pig (see p040). 'It's the place to take your significant other.'

In her free time, Kienle visits the Met Museum (see p024) to view 'some of our nation's greatest treasures', and browses W/17 (see p080) for accent pieces for the home, as well as LRI Design Plaza (see p080), 'a small concern with showrooms of artists and designers'. On Saturday mornings, she stops by Salcedo Market (Jaime Velasquez Park, T 895 4011) to buy homecooked delicacies before driving for two hours to the Anilao peninsula to go scuba-diving, or heading into the hills to Antonio's (see p096). 'It has a beautiful ambience, impeccable service and great food,' she says.
For full addresses, see Resources.

ARCHITOUR

A GUIDE TO MANILA'S ICONIC BUILDINGS

First impressions of Manila's US-influenced car and mall culture, and its rampant property speculation that often bulldozes history in its wake, tend to be negative. But amid the 1980s-style pastiches, pastels and aquamarine glass, there are many forgotten gems. Of the few buildings that survived WWII, seek out the Gothic revival all-steel Basilica of San Sebastian (Plaza del Carmen) by Genaro Palacios, assembled in 1891, and the art deco of Escolta Street (see p076), Juan Arellano's 1931 Metropolitan Theater (Padre Burgos Avenue) and the later ensemble seen at the Far Eastern University (Nicanor Reyes Street), by Pablo Antonio and Felipe Mendoza.

Postwar reconstruction was influenced by global modernism and produced some fine state (see p068) and private buildings (see p069). The accession of Ferdinand Marcos in 1965 coincided with a search for a national style, mining folk cultures for inspiration; the most extreme exponent is the Coconut Palace (F Ma Guerrero Street) by Francisco Mañosa, which features 47,000 shells and has roofs resembling *salakots* (traditional gourd hats). As governor of Manila, Imelda Marcos showed a megalomania and lack of regard for the common man that did, however, create a legacy of glorious buildings, courtesy of the genius at her disposal. Leandro Locsin left his mark all over town, especially in the CCP area (see p012), which Marcos raised from the sea to create her very own Atlantis. *For full addresses, see Resources.*

Zuellig Building

Loved by locals, Zuellig's reflective facade enables the 155m tower to almost vanish from certain angles. Designed by SOM, with WV Coscolluela & Associates, the glass curtain wall incorporates a ceramic frit pattern, inspired by bamboo and water, that helps control heat and light. Opened in 2012, it is the first office building in the country to be awarded an LEED platinum certificate. It recycles water, filters air and automatically dims lights, and a 2,500 sq m garden at street level reduces the carbon footprint. The bamboo design is replicated in the wood and marble lobby; from here, head on up to Asian fusion canteen Terraz on the third floor, or the Sky Garden (T 576 500; call in advance to visit) outside on the 32nd. Created by landscape architects EA Aurelio, it has superlative views of Makati.
Makati Avenue/Paseo de Roxas

Church of the Gesù

Recio+Casas' wholly modern Jesuit church overlooks the private Ateneo de Manila campus and quickly became an icon of the university. The tetrahedral form symbolises the Holy Trinity and the overhanging roof of a nipa hut. Yet the building is light, airy and transparent, with space for 1,000 and slanting walls of open louvres allowing views of the green surrounds, topped by a glass prism that is illuminated at night.

The crucifix above the altar is unusual in that it depicts Jesus still alive, looking up to God, rather than with his head bowed. The dedication in 2002 was attended by Cardinal Jaime Sin, which no doubt caused a few sniggers among the students. To visit, register at the front gate; also in the grounds is the 1963 Manila Observatory.
Ateneo de Manila University, Katipunan Avenue, T 426 6001, www.ateneo.edu

Ramon Magsaysay Building
WWII guerilla captain Ramon Magsaysay became the president of the Philippines in 1953, until his death in a plane crash in 1957, ruling over an era dubbed the 'Golden Years'. A foundation set up in his memory organises an annual awards showcase, now considered to be the Asian Nobel Prize, in this impressive 1967 building. Designed by Alfredo Luz, in consultation with US firms Pietro Belluschi and Alfred Yee Associates, the 18-storey tower is rooted by a central concrete core that allows lateral motion in case of earthquakes and typhoons. It also enables column-free floors, maximising space, which was perhaps an attraction for the CIA, which was rumoured to have an HQ here. Located on Roxas Boulevard, Manila's Lake Shore Drive, it stands out for its white travertine marble cladding.
1680 Roxas Boulevard, T 521 3166

Philamlife Building

Carlos Arguelles' 1961 HQ for the insurance giant is the zenith of International Style in Manila. Grey-tinted glass curtain walls are framed by a concrete grid with quartets of cantilevered planes forming brise-soleil. There's a colonnade at ground level and an expressive concrete canopy connects to the street. Within the building, an 800-seat narra-wood-panelled auditorium hosts classical music. Sadly, the property was sold to Henry Sy (see p073) in 2013, who will convert it into flats; the concert hall was saved after public protests led by the Philippines Philharmonic. Arguelles was prolific, designing gated estates, high-rise condos, banks and hotels, such as the 1968 Hilton (now the Waterfront Pavilion), opposite. Nearby is another fine modernist building, Alfredo Luz's WHO, from 1959.
United Nations Avenue

San Miguel Corporation Building
Green ahead of its time, this remarkable design by the Mañosa brothers (Francisco, Manuel and José), constructed from 1975 to 1984, was inspired by the Banaue Rice Terraces and has been dubbed Manila's Hanging Gardens of Babylon. It plugs into the Filipino vernacular, and embraces the now in the form of solar panelling, as well as one of the city's busiest heliports.
San Miguel Avenue

SM Aura Premier
Mall magnate Henry Sy went upmarket with this sculptural, layered L-shaped building with go-faster windows. It might resemble an oil tanker but eco-credentials include a landscaped roof park with water features and an egg-shaped 1,300-capacity concert hall. The obligatory chapel is designed like an abstract cave of the Resurrection.
McKinley Parkway, T 815 2872

Meralco Building

For the HQ of power company Meralco, Filipino architect José Maria Zaragoza delivered 14 concave storeys of hybrid International Style shielded by electric grill-like brise-soleil. An art deco-tinged basement theatre seats 1,000 and debuted just before the CCP (see p012) in 1969, with a gala show by the Bolshoi Ballet. It is still in use today.
Ortigas Avenue

Escolta Street

The city's oldest district outside Intramuros attracted merchants mainly from Fujian, selling goods from the galleon trade with Acapulco. In its heyday from the 1920s, Escolta had the capital's most modern buildings and boutiques, typified by Andrés Luna de San Pedro's 1932 art deco Crystal Arcade, which housed the stock exchange and Manila's first mall, and attracted the cream of society. All this was decimated in the war. Of the edifices that survived, many are abandoned, such as the art deco 1935 Capitol Theater (No 245), by Juan Nakpil, which has reliefs by Francesco Monti. Over the road is the Escolta Museum (No 266). Andrés Luna also designed the eclectic Regina Building (above; No 410), which dates to 1934 and housed offices of sugar and shipping firms. Its restoration has generated hope that more will follow.

GSIS Building

From afar, the GSIS looms like a beached cruiseliner, given its isolated setting by the water. Only on approach do you realise its scale – 125,400 sq m of social security HQ housing 4,000 workers (and 3,000 visitors) and, since 1997, the Philippines Senate. The multi-tiered concept is similar to that of San Miguel (see p070). Here, architects Jorge Ramos and TAC have created a 1981 prototype for energy-efficient architecture in a hot, humid climate. Its V shape widens towards the bay, funnelling the sea breeze. The staggered floors and planted terraces collect rainwater, open the building up to natural daylight and harness solar power, while overhangs provide shading – there is even a desalination plant. GSIS invested part of the state pension fund in art; book in advance to see the gallery (T 479 3588).
JW Diokno Boulevard

Two E-com Center

Manila is second only to Bangalore as the call-centre capital of the world, as locals speak English and are well-versed in US culture, having grown up watching its TV shows and eating Krispy Kremes. There are more than one-million employees in the Philippines – in Eastwood City mall, there's even a statue of faceless workers wearing headsets – who are well paid to do night shifts to align with US time. They hit the bar at dawn, giving local businesses a boost. Two E-com opened in 2011 as one of four purpose-built hubs at the Mall of Asia (see p092), offering 'lifestyle services for the 24/7 week'. Designed by the prolific Arquitectonica, with Felix S Lim, two perpendicular black-glass volumes appear to turn towards each other and connect via a sky bridge and a landscaped podium, Prism Plaza, used as an events space with alfresco eateries overlooking the bay.
Block 17, Mall of Asia Complex

SHOPPING
THE BEST RETAIL THERAPY AND WHAT TO BUY

The tropical climate has resulted in a multitude of malls that locals treat like parks (green space is scarce). Recently, mass-market has been superceded by lifestyle-oriented variants with better design, as found at Power Plant Mall (Rockwell Drive/Estrella Street, T 898 1702), Shangri-La Plaza's East Wing (EDSA/Shaw Boulevard, T 370 2500), SM Aura Premier (see p072) and Bonifacio High Street, inspired by US retail arcades such as LA's Third Street Promenade.

The upper level of Greenbelt 5 has a selection of Filipino talent, from knitwear at Tan-Gan (T 729 9042) to bespoke shoes at Gaupo (T 896 2662) and exquisite *miniaudières* at Celestina (T 729 9727), in addition to lifestyle emporiums Myth (T 757 0162) and AC+632 (T 758 2564). Shop for furniture at Triboa Bay Living (Suite 106, T 403 6281) and homewares at Heima (Suite 229, T 798 0027) in LRI Design Plaza (210 Nicanor Garcia Street), and Asian decor and antique pottery at W/17 (2241 Chino Roces Avenue, T 478 1717).

Head to Kultura Filipino (Mall of Asia, T 556 0417) for craftwork such as capiz-shell coasters or woven baskets, and Silahis Arts & Artifacts (744 Calle Real del Palacio, T 527 2111) to buy items from around the Philippines such as *bulol* statues from the mountains. Then again, many visitors to Manila simply make a beeline to the chaotic Greenhills Shopping Center (T 721 0572) to pick up bargain South Sea pearls and a knock-off Rolex from Hong Kong.

For full addresses, see Resources.

Ritual

This eco-conscious store carries fair-trade produce sourced from independent farms, much of it sold loose to reduce the use of plastic (there are sacks of Mindoro sea salt and muscovado sugar). Shelves are lined with jars and bottles, containing Don Papa rum, sorghum syrup and *tsokolate* (hot chocolate), as well as coloured soaps and wooden utensils. The homemade cinnamon dark cacao, and hibiscus and basil soda, are delicious. The shop retails like-minded brands such as Theo & Philo's beautifully packaged artisanal chocolate (above), and Katipunan craft ales. Open from Tuesday to Saturday, 12pm to 9pm, Ritual is one of the anchor tenants of The Collective, home to dozens of creative ventures including gig space B-Side.
Unit A, 7274 Malugay Street, San Antonio Village, T 400 4326, www.ritual.ph

Kish

Influential designer Ito Kish kickstarted the rebirth of this furniture-laden street. His stripped-down store has a cubist-style facade and a back garden that bathes the interior in light. Kish uses native materials and reinterprets Filipino craftsmanship: his 2012 'Gregoria Lounge' wooden chair was inspired by the balusters in traditional homes, and his 2014 collection referenced classic rattan-weaving but utilised PVC instead. Also on sale are indigenous talents such as Vito Selma, a Cebu designer who creates organic and geometric pieces that resemble mathematical models. Eclectic global finds – teak cabinets from Burma, ceramic bowls from Bali – are juxtaposed with global brands including Organic Modernism's midcentury-style furniture.
233 Nicanor Garcia Street, Bel-Air, T 896 8366, www.kish.ph

Silverlens Gallery

As the Filipino economy explodes, there's a burgeoning appetite for contemporary art, and galleries regularly launch in Manila. Isa Lorenzo founded Silverlens ahead of the curve in 2004, and it was the first to host photography-only exhibits. It now represents more than a dozen artists in various fields such as painting and collage; Maria Taniguchi, Patricia Perez Eustaquio and Dina Gadia all show internationally.

Architect Anna Sy designed the striking modernist shell, which has grown via a footbridge into two irregularly shaped rooms and a nook for small shows, as the area developed into a creative hub. Also recommended is the multidisciplinary 1335MABINI (see p037) in Ermita.
12th floor, YMC Building 2, 2320 Chino Roces Avenue Extension, T 816 0044, www.silverlensgalleries.com

Firma Manila

In the early part of the millennium, Malate was the locus of a dynamic design scene in which eclectic lifestyle boutique Firma was a driving force, mixing the exotic and the elegant, from ostrich-egg lamps to embroidered silk pillows. Its influence remains huge, especially as the partners went separate ways, resulting in a double reinvention. Firma in Greenbelt 3 (T 757 4009) carries international pieces and local accessory designers like Wynn Wynn Ong and Joyce Makitalo, whereas Firma Manila has reopened in an art deco block that's an incubator of talent. It has more of an Asian focus – look out for the range inspired by vintage Filipino cigarette labels, as well as its signature shell tassels, often incorporated into candelabras and lamps.
North Syquia, 1991 MH del Pilar Street, T 524 8740, www.firma.com.ph

House of Laurel

Fashion designer Rajo Laurel is a national treasure, creating flattering yet fashion-forward casual- and formalwear for all. His atelier in gentrifying Poblacion resembles a gallery due to its angular architecture, concrete walls and floors, and all-white finish – indeed, work by up-and-coming artists Eugenia Alcaide and Ryan Villamael is on display. Laurel has an eye for trends, but always features inventive silhouettes, signature draping and elegant details, as seen in the stylish split-thigh uniforms he conceived for Spiral (see p020). His store is a platform for other designers such as Ann Ong, known for her nature-inspired bags and jewellery. Laurel has also created a line of stationery and endorses products ranging from mattresses to ice cream.
6013 Villena Street/Mañalac Street,
T 895 5688, www.rajolaurel.com

SPORTS AND SPAS
WORK OUT, CHILL OUT OR JUST WATCH

Basketball was introduced by the YMCA in the first half of the 20th century, and has become an obsession, with courts and makeshift hoops everywhere, even in cemeteries. The PBA is not organised regionally, rather teams are named after company sponsors, and all are based in Manila; games are held at the Araneta Coliseum (General Araneta Avenue) and MOA Arena (see p092). The top players are often stopped on the street with shout-outs of 'Idol!'.

Boxing is also popular thanks to homegrown world champion Manny Pacquiao, and when he fights, Manila grinds to a halt. He has inspired an interest in boxing as a workout at gyms like Elorde (www.elordeboxinggym.com). Indeed, locals love an exercise fad. However, when you see hundreds of joggers shuffling around tiny Ayala Triangle Gardens, or running down the ramp outside CCP (see p012) but walking up the other side, it might seem as if the heart is in the right place, but it's not really pumping. Who cares? The CCP area is perfect for an architecturally inspired jog, as are the clean pavements (the fact there are usable pavements at all is a revelation) in Fort – fun runs are often held here at weekends.

You can't come to the Philippines without having a massage, of course – try The Spa at Mandarin Oriental (Makati Avenue, T 750 0968). Alternatively, The Spa (www.thespa.com.ph) has many branches; in true Filipino style, the one in Fort has lofts for parties.
For full addresses, see Resources.

CHI, The Spa
Located in the garden wing of the EDSA Shangri-La hotel, set beside lush tropical greenery surrounding an organic-shaped pool that creates a surprising oasis in bustling Ortigas, the 3,000 sq m CHI spa provides further respite. Signature CHI massages are offered alongside Chinese and Filipino healing, including *hilot* (based on ancient folk medicine) and *dagdagay* (a foot massage using bamboo sticks). There is also a yoga studio with drop-in classes. Alternatively, Le Spa at Sofitel (see p020) melds modern Western and traditional Filipino techniques in a soothing interior that combines water features, Philippine shell and darkwood; one of the couples suites has a huge bath and sundeck.
Fourth/fifth floor, EDSA Shangri-La, 1 Garden Way, Ortigas Center, T 633 8888, www.shangri-la.com/manila

Ronac Art Center
Sitting prominently on Ortigas Avenue is this unconventional building by Jagnus Design Studio, which, considering the intent to pay homage to mattress brand Uratex (owned by the same family), has been executed superbly well. The large grey block, dotted with uneven windows, symbolises the foam, a spiral staircase represents the mattress springs, and the cantilevered roof evokes an iron frame. Much more than a furniture showroom, this is a lifestyle space, with cafés, eateries, galleries, independent retail and, on the third floor, a sleek, sky-lit, geometrically designed gym (opposite). When squads from the PBA are not practising here, and if you can gather enough players together to form a team, it is open to the public.
424 Ortigas Avenue, Greenhills North, T 570 9815

Mall of Asia Arena
The self-proclaimed 'eyecon' seats up to 20,000 spectators on five levels and hosts many of the country's biggest basketball games, including showcases by NBA teams, as well as touring bands. Opened in 2012, and designed by Arquitectonica and local firm Jose Siao Ling, an elliptic volume rests on an inclined plinth, clad in glass-and-aluminium composite panels that allow light to seep through; the eye itself is a multimedia screen. Despite the arena's pizzazz, the beehive facade of the car park behind almost steals the limelight. Manila's other major stadium is Araneta Coliseum (see p088). Designed by Dominador Lugtu, it was inaugurated in 1960 as the largest covered arena in the world – the diameter of its dome is 108m. It has held numerous Manny Pacquiao fights, but is most famous for Ali and Frazier's 1975 Thrilla in Manila.
JW Diokno Boulevard, T 470 2222, www.mallofasia-arena.com

Club Intramuros Golf Course

Within a decade of occupation, the US had filled in the moat around Intramuros' 16th-century tufa walls and built a golf course. It opened in 1907 but didn't survive WWII, when the old Spanish colonial core was bombed to oust the Japanese. The par-66 course was redesigned by golf architect Andy Dye in 1995, who added interesting challenges including water hazards and out-of-bounds – one hole is a variation of the second at Carnoustie, Scotland, and another inspired by the island 17th at Sawgrass, Florida. There's also a leafy driving range right next to Fort Santiago, which dates from 1593. The 4.5km-long ramparts are a favourite place for a stroll at dusk, with views over the bay, the river, the art deco City Hall and its clocktower, and the National Museum (see p026).
Bonifacio Drive, T 526 1291

Manila Polo Club
During polo season (January to March), champagne flows freely as riders such as Brunei's Prince Jefri Bolkiah and Thai duty-free mogul Vichai Srivaddhanaprabha battle it out on the field. On a regular day, members make use of the tennis (above) and badminton courts, pools, gym and bowling alley. The club opened in 1950 and was renovated in 2009 by architects Asuncion Berenguer Inc, who contrasted wood and marble with classic and modern furniture and paintings. Visiting requires an invite, perhaps to one of the weddings or parties often held here. It is located beside the gated Forbes Park (you'll need a pass to drive through), an exclusive enclave of embassies, modernist bungalows and a few new-money monstrosities.
McKinley Road, Forbes Park, T 817 0951, www.manilapolo.com.ph

ESCAPES

WHERE TO GO IF YOU WANT TO LEAVE TOWN

It is almost an unwritten rule not to hold events in Manila at the weekend, as everybody travels out of town. Tagaytay is popular; 60km away in the Cavite hills, it has a cool breeze and views of Taal lake and its volcano. The cream of society dines at Antonio's (Purok 138, Barangay Neogan, T 917 899 2866) and plays golf at Tagaytay Highlands (Tagaytay-Calamba Road, T 46 483 0888). Stay at The Boutique Bed & Breakfast (45 Aguinaldo Highway, T 46 413 1798) or the contemporary T House (3195 Calamba Road, T 788 7354).

The beaches of Puerto Galera and Punta Fuego are only a few hours' drive from the capital, yet you'll reach the country's famed powder-fine sands in the same time by plane. Boracay has become quite a party isle, but quiet luxury can be found at Discovery Shores (Station 1, Balabag, T 720 8888) and the Shangri-La (see p102). There are also stunning spots near Cebu (see p100). Stay overnight at Abacá Boutique Resort (Punta Engano Road, T 32 236 0311) on Mactan Island, from where you can fly to Dedon Island (see p098), created by the global furniture brand's owner, Bobby Dekeyser.

Further west, Palawan is well-nigh undiscovered, and Puerto Princesa underground river, a UNESCO World Heritage Site, is one of its natural wonders. Wherever you go, scuba-diving is superb: favourite reefs are Malapascua, Tubbataha and Apo, for thresher sharks; Coron for WWII wrecks; and Oslob for whale sharks.
For full addresses, see Resources.

Ariara Island

Founded by British couple Charles and Carrie McCulloch, this 52-hectare resort in the Calamian archipelago has the feel of a super-luxe private home. Designed, by Filipino architect Jorge Yulo and Belgian Peter Ponnet, to have low environmental impact, the quartet of beach cottages with stunning sea views, two jungle villas built on stilts and two suites accommodate up to 18 guests. After yoga at sunrise, hire a boat to explore the surrounding wrecks and reefs. Dine in The Lodge at the end of the pier (above), and indulge in Swiss chef Jacqueline Alleje's Euro-Asian cuisine, or have a beach-party feast of *lechón*. Fly from Manila to Busuanga, then take a four-hour cruise to the island on Ariara's 30m trimaran, or eight guests can make the journey in an hour via speedboat. *Linapacan, Palawan, www.ariaraisland.com*

Dedon Island, Siargao

On the south-eastern tip of Siargao, this peaceful tropical island resort encourages a 'barefoot state of mind', which isn't hard to adopt when surrounded by mangrove forests, white sands and crystal waters. Created in collaboration with designers Jean-Marie Massaud and Daniel Pouzet, the villas, pavilions, pagodas and lounges are constructed using local materials and craftsmanship, balancing traditional architecture and modern features. Make the most of the all-inclusive, with massage, water sports and island-hopping boat trips on tap; or completely relax with a cocktail by the bar (right), or in the infinity pool, which transforms into an outdoor cinema in the evening. It takes just over an hour by plane from Manila to Cebu, from where you can catch a direct flight to Siargao, or charter a helicopter to arrive in style.
T 917 701 7820, www.dedonisland.com

ESCAPES

The Henry, Cebu
Opened in 2012, this 'design experience' in the nation's second city has a youthful, funky bent. Its airy environs persistently turn the head via its street- and pop-art decor, exposed interiors and opulent furnishings. The 38 rooms range from Big (pictured) to XX-Large, and the pool shimmers amid lush grass and lavender. *1 Paseo Saturnino, Maria Luisa Road, T 32 520 8877, www.thehenryhotel.com*

Shangri-La's Boracay Resort & Spa

The small island of Boracay lies roughly 350km south of Manila off the northern prong of the larger Panay. This near-flawless white-sanded idyll is known for its world-class beaches, array of water sports, nightlife and so many different ways to kick back it's almost stressful to contemplate. Relaxation options are only enhanced by the Shangri-La. Set among 12.5 hectares of gardens fronting a 350m private beach, the resort has 219 rooms, a range of restaurants and bars – from cliff-top to tree-top, beach or poolside – a spa and access to a nearby marine sanctuary. Book a Villa or Seaview Suite for personal butler service. To reach the hotel from Manila it's a 45-minute flight followed by a 15-minute transfer over land and sea.
Barangay Yapak, Boracay Island, T 36 288 4988, www.shangri-la.com/boracay

NOTES
SKETCHES AND MEMOS

RESOURCES
CITY GUIDE DIRECTORY

A

Abe Serendra 053
Serendra Plaza
T 856 0526

AC+632 080
Second floor
Greenbelt 5
Legaspi Street
T 758 2564

Antonio's 096
Purok 138
Barangay Neogan
Tagaytay
T 917 899 2866
www.antoniosrestaurant.ph

Aracama Filipino Cuisine 053
Unit C-1
The Fort Entertainment Center
T 917 861 2702
www.aracamamanila.com

Araneta Coliseum 088
General Araneta Avenue
www.aranetacoliseum.com

Art Informal 036
227 Connecticut Street
Greenhills East
T 725 8518
www.artinformal.com

Artelano 11 028
2680 FB Harrison Street
T 832 9972

Artlab Atelier Cesare and Jean Marie Syjuco 038
327 Country Club Drive
Ayala Alabang
T 917 534 0779

Avellena Art Gallery 029
2680 FB Harrison Street
T 833 8357

Ayala Museum 031
Greenbelt 4
Makati Avenue
T 759 8288
www.ayalamuseum.org

B

BAR 037
1335MABINI
1335 A Mabini Street
T 254 8498
www.1335mabini.com

Basilica of San Sebastian 064
Plaza del Carmen
T 735 8614

Black Market 060
Warehouse 5
La Fuerza/Compound 2
Sabio Street
T 908 813 5622

The Black Pig 044
Second floor
Commercenter Alabang
Commerce Avenue
Filinvest
Corporate City
T 808 1406
www.theblackpigbar.com

Black Sheep 039
Penthouse
W Fifth Avenue
32nd Avenue/5th Avenue
T 478 4498
www.blacksheepbgc.com

Blind Pig 040
227 Salcedo Street
T 917 549 2264

BSA Twin Towers 009
Julia Vargas Avenue

C

Capitol Theater 076
245 Escolta Street
T 241 4538

Caruso 062
21 Nicanor Garcia Street
T 895 2451

CAV 059
The Spa Building
Lot 5
Quadrant 8
Bonifacio High Street
T 856 1798
www.cavwine.com

Celestina 080
Ground floor
Greenbelt 5
Legaspi Street
T 729 9727
www.celestina.com.ph

CHI, The Spa 089
Fourth/fifth floor
EDSA Shangri-La
1 Garden Way
Ortigas Center
T 633 8888
www.shangri-la.com/manila

Church of the Gesù 066
Ateneo de Manila University
Katipunan Avenue
T 426 6001
www.ateneo.edu

Church of the Holy Sacrifice 024
University of the Philippines
Diliman
www.holysacrifice.net

Club Intramuros Golf Course 094
Bonifacio Drive
T 526 1291

La Cocina de Tita Moning 040
315 San Rafael Street
T 734 2141
www.lacocinadetitamoning.com

Coconut Palace 064
F Ma Guerrero Street

Craft Coffee Revolution 040
66 Broadway Avenue
T 570 3464

Cultural Center of the Philippines 012
Roxas Boulevard
www.culturalcenter.gov.ph

The Curator 041
134 Legaspi Street
T 917 893 7115

D

Discovery Primea 014
6749 Ayala Avenue
www.discoveryprimea.com

E

EDSA Beverage Design Group 041
CLMC Building
209 EDSA Greenhills
T 917 859 005
www.edsa-bdg.com

Escolta Museum 076
Second floor
Calvo Building
266 Escolta Street

Exit 040
Plaza Cafe
Corinthian Plaza
121 Paseo de Roxas
T 551 1283

F

Far Eastern University 064
Nicanor Reyes Street
www.feu.edu.ph

Finders Keepers 060
Black Market
Warehouse 5
La Fuerza/Compound 2
Sabio Street
T 555 5555

Firma 085
First floor
Greenbelt 3
Legaspi Street
T 757 4009

Firma Manila 085
Unit 12
North Syquia
1991 MH del Pilar Street
T 524 8740
www.firma.com.ph

Las Flores 054
One McKinley Place
25th Street/4th Avenue
T 552 2815

G

Gaupo 080
Second floor
Greenbelt 5
Legaspi Street
T 896 2662

Grace Park 046
One Rockwell Drive
T 843 7275

Greenhills Shopping Center 080
Ortigas Avenue
T 721 0572
www.greenhills.com.ph

GSIS Building 077
JW Diokno Boulevard

GSIS Gallery 077
GSIS Building
JW Diokno Boulevard
T 479 3588

H

Hatch 22 025
Power Plant Mall
Rockwell Drive/Estrella Street
T 915 109 7711

Heima 080
Suite 229
LRI Design Plaza
210 Nicanor Garcia Street
T 798 0027
www.heimastore.com

House of Laurel 086
6013 Villena Street/Mañalac Street
T 895 5688
www.rajolaurel.com

Hyve 056
Eighth floor
W Global Building
9th Avenue
T 917 633 5882

I

Iglesia ni Cristo 009
Commonwealth Avenue

J

Jojie Lloren atelier 029
2680 FB Harrison Street
T 556 4725

K
Kai 062
 Ground floor
 Greenbelt 5
 T 757 5209
Kenneth Cobonpue 032
 The Residences at Greenbelt
 San Lorenzo Tower
 Arnaiz Avenue
 T 576 1639
 www.kennethcobonpue.com
Kish 082
 233 Nicanor Garcia Street
 Bel-Air
 T 896 8366
 www.kish.ph
Kultura Filipino 080
 Mall of Asia
 T 556 0417
 www.kulturafilipino.com

L
LRI Design Plaza 080
 210 Nicanor Garcia Street
 T 895 1772
 www.lridesignplaza.com
Lusso 046
 Ground floor
 Greenbelt 5
 Legaspi Street
 T 756 5893

M
M Café 030
 Ground floor
 Greenbelt 4
 Makati Avenue
 T 757 6000
 www.raintreerestaurants.com

Malacañang Palace 024
 1000 JP Laurel Street
 T 784 4286
 www.malacanang.gov.ph
Mall of Asia Arena 092
 JW Diokno Boulevard
 T 470 2222
 www.mallofasia-arena.com
Manila Hotel 015
 One Rizal Park
 T 527 0011
 www.manila-hotel.com.ph
Manila Polo Club 095
 McKinley Road
 Forbes Park
 T 817 0951
 www.manilapolo.com.ph
Manila Post Office 010
 Magallanes Drive
Marikina Shoe Museum 024
 JP Rizal Street
 Santa Elena
 T 646 2368
Meralco Building 074
 Ortigas Avenue
Mesa Filipino Moderne 053
 SM Aura Premier
 C5 Road/26th Street
 T 815 2872
 www.mesa.ph
Metropolitan Museum 024
 Roxas Boulevard
 T 708 7828
 www.metmuseum.ph
Metropolitan Theater 064
 Padre Burgos Avenue

MO_Space 037
 MOS Design Building
 Bonifacio High Street
 T 856 2748
 www.mo-space.net
Myth 080
 Second floor
 Greenbelt 5
 Legaspi Street
 T 757 0162

N
National Museum 026
 Padre Burgos Drive
 Rizal Park
 T 527 0278
 www.nationalmuseum.gov.ph
Niner Ichi Nana 062
 The Globe Tower
 32nd Street
 T 917 876 9999
Ninyo Lounge 040
 66 Esteban Abada Street
 T 426 0301

O
1335MABINI 037
 1335 A Mabini Street
 T 254 8498
 www.1335mabini.com

P
People's Palace 058
 Ground floor
 Greenbelt 3
 T 729 2888
 www.peoplespalacethai.com

Pepita's Kithcen 024
 1050 Magallanes Avenue
 T 425 4605
Philamlife Building 069
 United Nations Avenue
Power Plant Mall 080
 Rockwell Drive/Estrella Street
 T 898 1702
 www.powerplantmall.com
Prime 101 047
 2226 Chino Roces Street
 T 720 8674
Privé Luxury Club 056
 Unit C
 The Fort Strip
 T 917 898 8181
 www.priveluxuryclub.com

Q
Quezon City Hall 011
 Elliptical Road
Quezon Memorial Circle 011
 Elliptical Road

R
Rambla 055
 Joya Building
 Joya Drive
 Rockwell Center
 T 823 6468
Ramon Magsaysay Building 068
 1680 Roxas Boulevard
 T 521 3166
 www.rmaf.org.ph
Recess by Chef Chris 057
 50 Jupiter Street
 Bel-Air
 T 899 1818

Red Box 056
Third floor
Greenbelt 3
Esperanza Street
T 757 6188
www.redbox.com.ph

Red Lantern 050
Solaire Resort & Casino
1 Asean Avenue
Entertainment City
T 888 8888
www.solaireresort.com

Regina Building 076
410 Escolta Street

Republiq 056
Unit 8
Second level
Newport Mall
Resorts World
T 917 550 8888

Ritual 081
Unit A
7274 Malugay Street
The Collective
San Antonio Village
T 400 4326
www.ritual.ph

Romulo Café 062
148 Jupiter Street
Bel-Air
T 478 6406

Ronac Art Center 090
424 Ortigas Avenue
Greenhills North
T 570 9815

S

71 Gramercy 042
The Gramercy Residences
Kalayaan Avenue/Salamanca Street
T 917 847 7535

Sala 058
Podium level
LV Locsin Building
6752 Ayala Avenue
T 750 5159
www.salarestaurant.com

Sala Bistro 058
Greenbelt 3
T 729 4888
www.salabistro.com

Salcedo Market 062
Jaime Velasquez Park
T 895 4011

San Miguel Corporation Building 070
San Miguel Avenue

Santo Niño de Paz Chapel 030
Greenbelt 4
Makati Avenue
T 729 8173
www.greenbeltchapel.org

Sarsa 040
Unit 1-7
Forum South Global
7th Avenue
T 927 706 0773

Shangri-La Plaza 080
EDSA/Shaw Boulevard
T 370 2500
www.shangrila-plaza.com

Silahis Arts & Artifacts 080
744 Calle Real del Palacio
T 527 2111

Silverlens Gallery 084
12th floor
YMC Building 2
2320 Chino Roces Avenue Extension
T 816 0044
www.silverlensgalleries.com

Sky Garden 065
32nd floor
Zuellig Building
Makati Avenue/Paseo de Roxas
T 576 500
www.zuelligbuilding.com

SM Aura Premier 072
McKinley Parkway
T 815 2872
www.sm-aura.com

Le Spa 020
Sofitel Philippine Plaza
CCP Complex
Roxas Boulevard
T 551 1587
www.sofitelmanila.com

The Spa at Mandarin Oriental 088
Mandarin Oriental
Makati Avenue
T 750 0968
www.mandarinoriental.com

SSS Building 011
East Avenue/Matapang Street

Strip 050
Solaire Resort & Casino
1 Asean Avenue
Entertainment City
T 888 8888
www.solaireresort.com

T
Tagaytay Highlands 096
Tagaytay-Calamba Road
Balangay
T 46 483 2033
www.tagaytayhighlands.com

Tan-Gan 080
Second floor
Greenbelt 5
Legaspi Street
T 729 9042
www.tan-gan.com

Triboa Bay Living 080
Suite 106
LRI Design Plaza
210 Nicanor Garcia Street
T 403 6281

Two E-com Center 078
Block 17
Mall of Asia Complex

U
University of the Philippines 024
Diliman
www.upd.edu.ph

US Military Cemetery 034
McKinley Road
T 844 0212

V
Vask 052
Fifth floor
CLIPP Center
11th Avenue/39th Street
T 217 6563
www.galleryvask.com

W
Wafu 048
 Greenhills Shopping Centre
 Ortigas Avenue
 T 570 3242
Wildflour Cafe + Bakery 051
 4th Avenue/26th Street
 T 856 7600
W/17 080
 Warehouse 17b
 La Fuerza Compound
 2241 Chino Roces Avenue
 T 478 1717
 www.w17home.com

Z
Zn Gallery 037
 1335MABINI
 1335 A Mabini Street
 T 254 8498
 www.1335mabini.com
Zuellig Building 065
 Makati Avenue/Paseo de Roxas
 www.zuelligbuilding.com

HOTELS
ADDRESSES AND ROOM RATES

Abacá Boutique Resort 096
Room rates:
double, from PHP19,400
Punta Engano Road
Mactan Island
Cebu
Lapu-Lapu
T 32 236 0311
www.abacaresort.com

Ariara Island 097
Room rates:
from PHP20,000 (minimum six guests)
Linapacan
Palawan
www.ariaraisland.com

The Boutique Bed & Breakfast 096
Room rates:
double, from PHP7,000
45 Aguinaldo Highway
Tagaytay
T 46 413 1798
www.theboutiquebnb.com

Dedon Island 098
Room rates:
double, from PHP70,000
Siargao
T 917 701 7820
www.dedonisland.com

Discovery Primea 014
Room rates:
suite, prices on request
6749 Ayala Avenue
T 955 8888
www.discoveryprimea.com

Discovery Shores 096
Room rates:
double, from PHP25,650
Station 1
Balabag
Boracay Island
T 720 8888
www.discoveryshoresboracay.com

The Henry 100
Room rates:
double, from PHP6,000;
Big Room, from PHP6,000;
XX-Large Room, PHP12,000
1 Paseo Saturnino
Maria Luisa Road
Cebu
T 32 520 8877
www.thehenryhotel.com

Joya Lofts 019
Room rates:
double, from PHP8,250
28 Plaza Drive
Rockwell Center
T 798 0497
www.hii-joya.com

Makati Shangri-La 016
Room rates:
double, from PHP14,700
Ayala Avenue/Makati Avenue
T 813 8888
www.shangri-la.com

Marco Polo 016
Room rates:
double, from PHP13,250
Meralco Avenue/Sapphire Street
T 720 7777
www.marcopolohotels.com

Nobu 016
Room rates:
prices on request
City of Dreams
T 866 9888
www.nobuhotels.com

The Peninsula 023
Room rates:
double, from PHP19,500;
Deluxe Suite, from PHP41,100
Ayala Avenue/Makati Avenue
T 887 2888
www.peninsula.com/manila

Picasso Boutique Serviced Apartments 018
Room rates:
double, from PHP9,000;
Picasso Loft, PHP15,000
119 LP Leviste Street
T 828 4774
www.picassomakati.com

Raffles 022
Room rates:
double, from PHP18,750
1 Raffles Drive
Makati Avenue
T 555 9777
www.raffles.com/makati

Shangri-La's Boracay Resort & Spa 102
Room rates:
double, from PHP30,650;
Seaview Suite, from PHP46,100;
Villa, from PHP54,050
Barangay Yapak
Boracay Island
T 36 288 4988
www.shangri-la.com/boracay

Sofitel Philippine Plaza 020
Room rates:
double, from PHP13,500;
Corner Suite, PHP22,800
CCP Complex
Roxas Boulevard
T 551 5555
www.sofitelmanila.com

Solaire Resort & Casino 017
Room rates:
double, from PHP8,000;
Chairman's Villa, from PHP366,000
1 Asean Avenue
Entertainment City
T 888 8888
www.solaireresort.com

T House Tagaytay 096
Room rates:
double, from PHP4,700
3195 Calamba Road
Tagaytay
T 788 7354
www.thousetagaytay.com

WALLPAPER* CITY GUIDES

Executive Editor
Rachael Moloney

Editor
Jeremy Case
Author
Cheryl Tiu

Art Editor
Eriko Shimazaki
Original Design
Loran Stosskopf

Photography Editor
Elisa Merlo
Assistant Photography Editor
Nabil Butt

Chief Sub-Editor
Nick Mee
Sub-Editor
Farah Shafiq

Editorial Assistant
Emilee Jane Tombs

Interns
Laura Hartung
Jose Rico Perez

Contributor
Kissa Castañeda

Wallpaper* ® is a registered trademark of IPC Media Limited

First published 2014

© Phaidon Press Limited

All prices are correct at the time of going to press, but are subject to change.

Printed in China

Phaidon Press Limited
Regent's Wharf
All Saints Street
London N1 9PA

Phaidon Press Inc
65 Bleecker Street
New York, NY 10012

Phaidon® is a registered trademark of Phaidon Press Limited

www.phaidon.com

A CIP Catalogue record for this book is available from the British Library.

All rights reserved. No part of this publication may be reproduced, stored in a retrieval system or transmitted, in any form or by any means, electronic, mechanical, photocopying, recording or otherwise, without the prior permission of Phaidon Press.

ISBN 978 0 7148 6832 5

PHOTOGRAPHERS

Pierre-Emmanuel Michel
Manila city view,
inside front cover
Manila Post Office, p010
Quezon Memorial
Circle, p011
Cultural Center of the
Philippines, pp012-013
Discovery Primea, p014
Manila Hotel, p015
Solaire Resort &
Casino, p017
Picasso Boutique Serviced
Apartments, p018, p019
Sofitel Philippine
Plaza, pp020-021
Raffles, p022
The Peninsula, p023
Hatch 22, p025
National Museum,
pp026-027
Artelano 11, p028, p029
M Café, p030
Ayala Museum, p031
Kenneth Cobonpue,
p032, p033
US Military Cemetery,
pp034-035

Art Informal, pp036-037
Artlab Atelier Cesare and
Jean Marie Syjuco, p038
Black Sheep, p039
The Curator, p041
71 Gramercy, pp042-043
The Black Pig, p044, p045
Grace Park, p046
Prime 101, p047
Wafu, pp048-049
Strip, p050
Wildflour Cafe +
Bakery, p051
Vask, p052
Mesa Filipino
Moderne, p053
Las Flores, pp054-055
Privé Luxury Club, p056
Recess by Chef Chris, p057
Sala, p058
CAV, p059
Black Market, pp060-061
Jessica Kienle, p063
Zuellig Building, p065
Church of the Gesù,
pp066-067
Ramon Magsaysay
Building, p068
Philamlife Building, p069
San Miguel Corporation
Building, pp070-071
SM Aura Premier,
pp072-073

Meralco Building,
pp074-075
Regina Building, p076
GSIS Building, P077
Two E-com Center,
pp078-079
Kish, p082, p083
Silverlens Gallery, p084
Firma Manila, p085
House of Laurel,
pp086-087
CHI, The Spa, p089
Ronac Art Center,
p090, p091
Mall of Asia Arena,
pp092-093
Club Intramuros Golf
Course, p094
Manila Polo Club, p095

Peartree Digital
Theo & Philo
chocolate, p081

MANILA
A COLOUR-CODED GUIDE TO THE HOT 'HOODS

MAKATI
A forest of towers houses the most prestigious hotels, banks, offices and living spaces

QUEZON CITY
Located just 15km north-east of Intramuros, Quezon's wide avenues seem a world apart

BINONDO/QUIAPO
On the Pasig's north bank, these shabby quarters contain fascinating vestiges of the past

PASAY/MALL OF ASIA
This stretch used to be underwater but is now a showcase for Locsin's eloquent brutalism

FORT
Developed in the 1990s on former army land, Fort is a breath of fresh air in the chaos

INTRAMUROS/RIZAL PARK
Have a sundowner on the Bayleaf hotel's rooftop to survey the colonial city as dusk falls

ORTIGAS
The bustling business hub never sleeps thanks to armies of call centre workers on nights

ERMITA/MALATE
Once the centre of Manila's raucous nightlife, this area is rediscovering its creative side

For a full description of each neighbourhood, see the Introduction.
Featured venues are colour-coded, according to the district in which they are located.